This book belongs to:

_____

It was given to me by:

_____

On:

_____

Bible
Prayers
for Bedtime

JANE LANDRETH
ILLUSTRATED BY RICHARD HOIT

BARBOUR BOOKS
An Imprint of Barbour Publishing, Inc.

ISBN 978-1-60260-066-9

Manuscript written and prepared in association with Snapdragon Group℠ Tulsa, Oklahoma, USA.

Published by Barbour Books, an imprint of Barbour Publishing, Inc., P. O. Box 719, Uhrichsville, Ohio 44683, www.barbourbooks.com

Our mission is to publish and distribute inspirational products offering exceptional value and biblical encouragement to the masses.

 Member of the
Evangelical Christian
Publishers Association

Printed in China.
05031 0715 DS

With love to my precious
grandsons,
Lane and Cody,
who bring joy and fulfillment
to our lives.

Jesus said,
"Let the little children come to me,
and don't prevent them.
For of such is the Kingdom of Heaven."
And he put his hands on their heads
and blessed them.

Matthew 19:14 TLB

Contents

The First Prayers

That's when men and women
began praying and worshiping
in the name of GOD.

Genesis 4:26 THE MESSAGE

A long time ago, God created the world. He made plants and birds and fish and animals. And then He made people. The first people were named Adam and Eve.

Adam and Eve lived in a beautiful garden called Eden. God talked with Adam and Eve in the garden. It was a perfect place. But then Adam and Eve did something wrong. They disobeyed God by eating fruit from a special tree. God had said, "Don't!"

Because they did wrong, God made Adam and Eve leave their beautiful garden. Now they had to work hard for their food. God told them that someday they would die. The wrong they did messed up everything!

Before long, Adam and Eve started a family. They had a baby boy they named Cain. Then they had another baby boy they called Abel. When the boys grew up, the wrong that Adam and Eve did caused more trouble. Cain got mad at his younger brother and killed him.

People could see that doing wrong things was a big problem. They knew that they needed help. And they knew that only God could help them.

So they started to call out to God. They asked Him for help. They prayed the first prayers. And people have been praying to God ever since.

Dear God, I'm so glad that I can talk to You. Thank You for listening to my prayers! Amen.

Praying for Your Family

Isaac's wife could not have children,
so Isaac prayed to the LORD for her.
The LORD heard Isaac's prayer.

Genesis 25:21 NCV

God wants us to pray for each of our family members—Mom, Dad, sisters and brothers, grandparents, aunts and uncles, and cousins. Isaac asked God to give his wife, Rebekah, something she wanted—children. And God heard his prayer.

Isaac knew that Rebekah wanted a child. No one knew why, but she had not had any babies. Abraham, Isaac's father, loved and worshipped God. He taught Isaac to pray to God about everything. So he prayed. "God, Rebekah is a good wife. I love her very much. Would You please give her what she wants most—a baby of her own?"

God answered Isaac's prayer in a special way. Soon Rebekah learned that she was going to have a baby. And not just one but two! She was going to have twins. She could tell because she could feel them tumbling around inside her.

Soon the day came when Rebekah had the babies. First came one boy. Isaac and Rebekah named him Esau. Then came another boy. They named him Jacob. The boys grew. Isaac and Rebekah were happy with their new family. Isaac thanked God for answering his prayer.

Dear heavenly Father, thank
You for my family—Mom, Dad,
sisters, and brothers.
Help me remember to pray
for each one of them every day.
Amen.

"Deliver Me from Destruction"

O Lord, please deliver me from
destruction at the hand of my brother
Esau, for I am frightened—
terribly afraid that he is coming
to kill me.

Genesis 32:11 TLB

When we are afraid someone will hurt us, we can pray. Jacob asked God to keep him safe when he was afraid his brother, Esau, would hurt him.

One day Jacob stole something important from his brother. He knew that Esau wanted to hurt him for that—so Jacob ran away.

Many years later, God told Jacob to go back home. Jacob and his family packed their things for the long trip. Jacob sent some helpers to tell Esau that he wanted to come home for a visit.

The helpers came back and said, "We saw Esau. He is coming to meet you with four hundred men!"

Jacob was afraid. Four hundred men sounded like an army! So Jacob prayed for God to keep him and his family safe.

Jacob decided to send Esau some presents. After all, he was the one who had stolen from Esau.

Step, step, step! Jacob and his family walked. Finally, they saw Esau and his four hundred men coming!

As Jacob walked toward Esau, he bowed over and over to show he was sorry for the wrong things he had done. Esau ran toward Jacob. Jacob wondered if Esau was going to hurt him. But Esau grabbed Jacob and gave him a hug.

Heavenly Father, thank You for
keeping me safe when
someone wants to hurt me.
Help me remember that You will
always take care of me.
Amen.

A Special Piece of Wood

Moses cried out to the LORD,
and the LORD showed him a piece
of wood.
Exodus 15:25

When we need help with a problem, we can pray. Even when Moses and God's people were in the desert without water, God answered Moses' cry for help.

Have you ever been hot and thirsty? Long ago, God's people were hot and thirsty. They could not find a drop of cool water to drink.

God's people were on a long trip. They walked through the hot desert. There were very few trees for shade. There was no water to drink, but there was a lot of hot sand. God's people walked across the hot, hot sand. Step, step, step!

For three days, God's people had no water. "We are thirsty!" they grumbled to Moses, their leader.

Then someone shouted, "Water!"

The people saw the clear, cool water. They ran to it and took big drinks.

"Yuck! This water tastes bad," they complained. "We can't drink this water."

Moses heard the grumbling people. He asked God what to do. God told Moses to throw a special piece of wood into the water. *Splash!*

The special piece of wood made the water taste good. Everyone began to drink, slowly at first. They drank faster as they realized how good it tasted.

Moses was happy. God had showed him what to do to help the thirsty people.

Dear God, thank You for giving me cool water to drink. Help me to pray when I have a problem. I know You will always answer my prayer.

Amen.

Water from a Rock

Moses cried out to the LORD,
"What am I to do with these people?"
Exodus 17:4

When someone wants to argue with us, we can pray and ask God what He wants us to do. God's people argued with Moses, and he talked to God about all their arguing and complaining.

God had chosen Moses to lead the people to a new land. He had guarded them from the great armies that wanted to destroy them. God had given them food when they were hungry. Now they were in the desert.

"Give us water to drink," the people demanded.

"Why are you always arguing with me?" asked Moses. "Don't you know God will take care of us?"

But the people kept shouting.

Moses talked to God. "What do You want me to do?" he prayed.

God answered Moses and said, "Walk ahead of the people. Take some of the older leaders with you. Take the staff with you. When you come to a big rock, strike the rock with your staff. Water will come out of the rock."

So Moses did what God told him to do. When the people came to the rock, there was fresh water for them to drink. Moses was thankful that God heard his prayer and gave the people what they needed.

Dear God, tell me what to do
when people around me argue
and grumble. Help me tell them
that You love them and can
make them happy.
Amen.

"Help Me to Know You, Lord"

"If you are pleased with me,
teach me more about yourself.
Then I can know you.
And I can continue to please you."

Exodus 33:13 NIRV

When you want to know about your friend, you spend time with that friend. By spending time in prayer, you can learn more about God. Moses wanted to know more about God so he spent more time praying to Him. That's when God told Moses about the important things He wanted Moses to do.

Moses led God's people away from the king of Egypt, who was unkind to them. Moses asked God to give the people fresh water to drink when they were thirsty. He asked God for food to eat when they were hungry. God gave Moses the Ten Commandments to help the people know how they could please God.

After Moses heard about all the things God wanted him to do, he spent even more time talking to God. He wanted to know more so that he could please God in everything he did.

Whenever Moses had a problem, he talked to God about it. God always helped him know what to do. Moses became a very great leader. All the people respected him and listened to him. Even the king of Egypt listened. He didn't want to, but he finally let God's people follow Moses.

God, just like Moses, I want to know You. Help me spend more time with You in prayer. Thank You for always being near me. Amen.

Loud Horns and Broken Walls

Joshua fell with his face to the ground.
He asked the man, "What message does
my Lord have for me?"

Joshua 5:14 NIRV

Sometimes when we pray, God tells us to do something. And sometimes what He tells us seems strange. When Joshua and God's people prayed, God told them to do something very strange. But they trusted Him and obeyed Him.

"We need God's help," Joshua said when he saw the great walls around the city of Jericho. Joshua prayed and God spoke to him.

"I want you to capture this city," God said. "The people there will know about Me."

Joshua listened to God's plan. Then he told the people what to do.

"Do what?" the people said.

"God wants us to march around

the city," Joshua said. "All the priests should go first and keep blowing their horns. The rest of us will follow. Every day for six days, we will all march around the city once. Don't say a word until I tell you."

Finally on the seventh day, the people marched around Jericho, one, two, three, four, five, six, and seven times. Then the horns blew loud!

Joshua said, "Shout really loud, everyone!"

All the people shouted at once.

Then *crash! Boom! Bang!* The great walls of Jericho fell down flat! God did an impossible thing that no one else could do.

God, sometimes I don't
understand why You want me to
do something. But I will
just obey. You always know
what is right for me.
Amen.

"Sun, Stand Still"

Joshua stood before
all the people of Israel
and said to the LORD,
"Sun, stand still over Gibeon."

Joshua 10:12 NCV

Sometimes we need to pray for a miracle when we have something hard to do. Joshua prayed for a miracle in a hard time. Five great kings and their armies were fighting against Joshua's one small army.

Could Joshua's army beat so many soldiers all at once? Joshua stopped right where he was to ask God what he should do. He prayed for a long, long time. God told him, "Go, fight. I will help you."

Joshua sounded the alarm. "Get ready to march!"

Tramp, tramp, tramp! Up the hills and down the valleys, Joshua led his little army. The soldiers went right to where the five great armies were camping.

The enemy armies were so surprised that they ran into the mountains.

Joshua's army followed the enemy soldiers into the mountains. They needed to find them, or they would come back to fight again. But it was getting dark!

God knew Joshua's army needed more daylight. So God put an idea into Joshua's mind.

Joshua stood up and said, "Sun, stand still!" The sun stopped moving! It did not go down until all the enemy soldiers were captured. No one had ever seen a miracle like that before—or since.

Dear God, thank You for giving me a miracle when I must do hard things. Help me to remember that You are always near when I need Your help.

Deborah's Song of Praise

"Let all the people who love you
be as strong as the rising sun!"
Judges 5:31 NCV

Praising God is an important part of praying. Deborah sang a song of praise to God when He helped her people fight against a great army.

Deborah was God's prophet. She told people God's messages. Deborah was also a judge. She sat under a large tree and listened to people who had problems and needed her help.

One day, God gave Deborah a special message. He told her to call for a mighty soldier named Barak. Deborah told him, "God wants you to take your army to Mount Tabor. He is going to help you fight against the great army that is trying to hurt our people."

Barak thought about the great

army's strong soldiers and iron chariots. He felt afraid. "Will you go with us?" he asked Deborah.

"I will," said Deborah.

Deborah went with Barak and his soldiers to Mount Tabor, just like God had told them to do.

The great army with its iron chariots and strong soldiers fought against Barak and his men. But God was the strongest. He helped Barak and his men win the battle.

Deborah was so happy that she sang a praise song to God.

Dear God, thank You so much for loving me and keeping me safe. Help me keep singing praises to You because I love You and want to worship You. Amen.

"Give Me a Sign"

Gideon replied,
"If you are pleased with me,
give me a special sign. Then I'll know
that it's really you talking to me."
Judges 6:17 NIRV

If we don't understand what God is saying to us, we need to ask again. In the Bible, God sometimes gave His people special signs. That way, they would know for sure that it was God speaking to them. That is what happened to Gideon.

One day, an angel said to Gideon, "The Lord is with you. Gather together some soldiers because a strong army is coming to fight you."

Gideon wanted to be sure it was God who had spoken. So he prayed, "God, give me a special sign. Tonight, I will lay a piece of wool on the floor. In the morning, if the wool is wet and the floor is dry, I will know You are sending me to fight. I will know that You will help us to win."

The next morning, Gideon hurried to the wool. The wool was so wet that Gideon squeezed out water. He looked at the floor and it was dry.

Again Gideon prayed. "God, don't be angry with me, but I want to be really, really sure. This time, make the wool dry and the floor wet."

The next morning, the wool was dry and the floor was wet.

Now Gideon was ready to obey God.

Dear God, thank You for the
Bible that tells me how You
answer prayers. Help me to
know in my heart when
You are speaking to me.
Amen.

"Remember Me"

[Hannah] made a promise, saying,
"LORD All-Powerful, see how sad I am.
Remember me and don't forget me.
If you will give me a son,
I will give him back to you all his life."

1 Samuel 1:11 NCV

Sometimes we make promises to God when we pray. Hannah made a promise—and she kept it.

Hannah had been married for a long time, but she had no children. She wanted a child more than anything in the world. One day, Hannah was in the temple praying. The old priest Eli saw her.

He could hear her crying quietly. He saw her lips move as she prayed to God. He could tell that she was very sad.

"What is wrong?" he asked.

"I am sad," answered Hannah. "I have been asking God to help me."

"I will pray for you," said Eli. "May

God answer your prayers and give you what you ask."

Later, God did answer Hannah's prayers. She had a baby boy and named him Samuel. Baby Samuel grew and grew.

"I must keep my promise to God," said Hannah. She took Samuel to the temple and showed him to Eli.

"Do you remember the day I was here praying?" she asked. "I wanted God to give me a child. Now here he is! It's time to keep my promise. Samuel will be here in the temple to help you whenever you need him."

Hannah praised God for remembering her prayer.

God, thank You for
answering my prayers.
Help me not to make promises
that I cannot keep,
and help me keep
the promises I do make.
Amen.

"Speak to Me, Lord"

Samuel said,
"Speak, for your servant is listening."
1 Samuel 3:10

Praying isn't always talking to God. Sometimes we need to be quiet and listen. Young Samuel learned to listen to God.

Samuel yawned and stretched his arms. He was sleepy, so he lay down and closed his eyes. Then something strange happened. Samuel heard someone call.

"Samuel! Samuel!"

He jumped out of bed and ran to where Eli, the priest, slept. "You called me, and here I am," Samuel said.

Eli looked surprised. "I did not call you," he said. "Go back to bed."

Samuel went back to bed. Everything was quiet. Then he heard the voice again.

"Samuel! Samuel!"

Samuel hurried to Eli. "Here I am. Did you call me?" he asked.

"No," said Eli. "I did not call you. Go back to bed."

Samuel was just closing his eyes when he heard the voice again.

"Samuel! Samuel!"

He ran to Eli for the third time. "Here I am. Did you call me?"

Then Eli knew God was calling Samuel. "When you hear the voice again," Eli told Samuel, "say, 'Speak to me, God. I am listening.' "

Soon Samuel heard the voice again.

"Samuel! Samuel!"

Samuel said, "Speak to me, God. I am listening."

Then something wonderful happened. God spoke to Samuel. And Samuel listened carefully to all God told him.

Dear God, thank You for listening to the things I want to tell You. Help me to be quiet and listen to the things You want to tell me.
Amen.

"Don't Stop Praying"

They said to Samuel,
"Don't stop praying to the
LORD our God for us!"
1 Samuel 7:8 NCV

We can pray when people try to hurt us. The people asked Samuel to keep praying when their enemy tried to fight them. God answered Samuel's prayer.

Samuel told the people of Israel to worship and serve God. But they did not listen to him. They did not obey God. Because of this, a great army came to fight with them.

Samuel was sad. He told the people, "God wants you to obey Him. Begin to worship and serve God. He will save you from great armies like this one!"

This time the people listened to Samuel. They got together in the city to pray and worship God.

The leaders of the great army saw them in the middle of the town. They told the army to move forward and fight against them.

The people were afraid. They said to Samuel, "Don't stop praying for God to help us. Keep praying." Samuel prayed that God would help them fight and win.

Bang! Crash! God made a loud clap of thunder. It scared the great army, and the soldiers ran away. The people of Israel knew God had helped them.

Dear God in heaven, thank You
for keeping me safe. When
someone wants to hurt me,
help me remember to pray.
Help me worship and obey You.
Amen.

A New King

Samuel wasn't pleased when they said,
"Give us a king to lead us."
So he prayed to the Lord.

1 Samuel 8:6 NIRV

We can pray when something is bothering us. Samuel was unhappy when the people said they wanted a king. He knew that God wanted to be their king. He knew he should talk to God about it.

"We want a king!" the people were shouting. "We want a king like the other countries."

So Samuel prayed.

After Samuel prayed, God spoke to him. "Give the people what they want. Tomorrow you will meet a man who will be the next king."

The next day, Saul came to see Samuel. Saul did not know Samuel was looking for anyone. Saul did not know that he would become the king.

When Samuel saw Saul, God said to Samuel, "This is the man I told you about."

That night, Samuel gave Saul a special place of honor at the evening meal.

The next morning Samuel took Saul to the edge of the city. He took oil and poured it over Saul's head. This meant that God had chosen Saul to be king.

Later Samuel gathered the people together. "Here is your new king," he said.

Dear God, thank You for helping me when something is bothering me. Help me remember that You will always give me an answer. Amen.

When God Says "No"

"Lord and King, how great you are!
There isn't anyone like you.
There isn't any God but you."

2 Samuel 7:22 NIRV

God doesn't always give us everything we pray for. Sometimes He says "no," just like He did to King David.

After David became king, he dreamed of building a beautiful temple. David wanted a place where God's people could gather to worship Him.

God was glad about King David's idea. He told David just how the temple should be built. He told him to get everything ready for the builders. God even told King David what the people could do to help. They gathered wood, stone, and cloth to use in the beautiful temple.

Then God told King David something else. "I have not chosen you to build the temple. I have chosen your son Solomon to build it."

King David could have been sad and upset that he would not be the one to build the beautiful temple. But instead, he was thankful that God had chosen Solomon. He was thankful that the people would have a wonderful place to worship God.

King David prayed a prayer of thanksgiving. "Thank You so much for blessing me and for blessing Your people. You are great, O God. There is no one else like You."

Thank You, God, for not giving me everything I ask for. You know what I need much better than I do. Help me to be thankful when You say "no." Amen.

Keep Praying

[Elijah] bent down toward the ground.
Then he put his face between his knees.

1 Kings 18:42 NIRV

Sometimes God answers our prayers quickly, and sometimes we must keep praying. Elijah had to keep praying for a long, long time before God answered his prayer.

The ground was dry. There was no green grass. The rivers had no water. Not a drop of rain fell!

One day, God told Elijah, "I will send rain."

Elijah and his helper climbed to the top of a mountain. Elijah bowed his head and talked to God.

After Elijah prayed, he told his helper, "Go and look toward the ocean. See if there are any clouds."

The helper ran to look. "I don't see

any clouds," he said.

Elijah prayed again. The helper looked toward the ocean—but still no clouds.

Elijah prayed again. He asked his helper to look two, three, four, five, six more times. But still there were no clouds. Elijah kept praying.

"Go look one more time," said Elijah.

This time, Elijah's helper saw something—about the size of a man's hand. Could it be a cloud? Yes! It was a small cloud!

The cloud grew bigger and bigger. The sky became dark and the winds blew. *Pitter-patter, pitter-patter!* The rain fell on the dry ground. God finally answered Elijah's prayer.

Thank You, God, for sending rain to make the world beautiful and provide water for the animals to drink. Help me to keep praying for things I need, just like Elijah did.

Amen.

Behind Closed Doors

Elisha went into the room.
He shut the door. He was alone with
the boy. He prayed to the Lord.
2 Kings 4:33 NIRV

Many times we pray with other people—like at home or church. But sometimes God wants us to pray alone, just like Elisha did.

Elisha traveled around telling people about God. Many times, Elisha visited a man and woman who had no children. Since Elisha came to the city often, the couple built a room for him to stay in. Because of their kindness toward Elisha, God blessed the couple with a son.

One day, while the son was in the field with his father, he became very sick.

His father brought him to the house. His mother carried him into Elisha's room and laid him on the bed. Then she hurried to find Elisha.

When Elisha saw the woman coming, he knew something was wrong. Immediately, they hurried back to the house. Elisha went into the room and closed the door. He was alone with the boy. Then he prayed.

Elisha lay on the bed with the boy. Then he walked back and forth across the room. Suddenly the boy sneezed one, two, three, four, five, six, seven times, and opened his eyes. The boy's parents were very happy. Elisha's prayers had been answered.

Dear God, thank You for
letting me pray with others.
But help me to remember that
You also would like to have some
time alone with me.
Amen.

"Deliver Us"

"Now, O LORD our God,
deliver us from his hand,
so that all kingdoms on earth may know
that you alone, O LORD, are God."
2 Kings 19:19

When someone wants to hurt us, we can ask God to keep us safe. When Hezekiah got a letter saying a great army was coming to destroy his land, he prayed and asked God to keep his people safe.

Hezekiah was a good king. He loved and respected God, and he told his people to worship God, too. God blessed him. Hezekiah and his army began to win all their battles. Each time they won a battle, Hezekiah would thank God for helping them.

One day Hezekiah got a letter from Sennacherib, a king from another country. Sennacherib said he and his army were strong and would destroy Hezekiah and his army. He said that God would not help Hezekiah.

When Hezekiah got the letter, he went to the temple and spread the letter out in front of him. He prayed to God.

"You are the only God," said Hezekiah. "We are in trouble. Sennacherib has a strong army. We need help. Save us from the powerful Sennacherib. Show him and his soldiers that You are the only God."

God heard Hezekiah's prayer and took care of the great army for them.

Dear God in heaven, thank You
for keeping me safe when
someone wants to hurt me.
Help me remember that You can
help me when I am in trouble.
Amen.

"Enlarge My Territory"

Jabez cried out to the God of Israel,
"Oh, that you would bless me and
enlarge my territory!"
1 Chronicles 4:10

Sometimes we say long prayers and sometimes we say short prayers. Jabez said a very short prayer. But it was a powerful prayer.

When Jabez was young, he heard about God. He heard how God rescued His people from great armies and placed them in a land He had promised them. Jabez knew that God would hear him, even if he prayed a short prayer.

Jabez asked God to bless him. He knew God wanted to give him many good things, but he also knew he had to ask for them.

Jabez asked God to "enlarge his territory." This meant that he wanted to tell more people about God.

Jabez knew he needed God to be near him at all times. Sometimes things were hard for him, and he needed God to help him. He asked God to give him kind words to say and to help him do right things.

Then he asked God to keep him away from the bad things that might hurt him.

When he prayed for these things, God answered him and gave him the things he wanted. God blessed Jabez's friends and family—all because Jabez wanted to please God in all he did and said.

Dear God, help me pray like
Jabez. Bless me every day.
Help me tell people about You.
Be near me at all times and keep
bad things away from me.
Amen.

"Give Me Wisdom"

"Give me wisdom and knowledge,
that I may lead this people."
2 Chronicles 1:10

Sometimes we ask God for things like a shiny bicycle, a pretty doll, or some new clothes. Solomon didn't ask God for things. He only wanted God to make him wise.

When Solomon became king, he prayed for God to help him. "Give me wisdom and knowledge, that I may lead the people," he prayed.

The people were happy because they knew King Solomon worshipped God. And he was wise enough to know what the people needed. One of the first things King Solomon did was help the people build the temple. It was a grand church where they could worship God.

All the people worked on the temple. *Bang, bang!* Hammers hit the stone. *Zzzz, zzzz!* Saws cut the wood. It took a long, long time.

Finally, the temple was finished. It was very, very beautiful.

King Solomon planned a special party to thank God for the temple. When the people arrived, King Solomon got down on his knees and held his hands up toward heaven.

King Solomon began to pray to God. "There is no other God like You in heaven or on earth," he said. He thanked God for making him wise and for giving God's people such a beautiful place to worship.

Dear God, thank You for all the things You have given me. Help me to pray for Your help when I have choices to make. Help me to be wise.
Amen.

"We Trust in You"

Asa called out to the Lord his God.
He said, "Lord, there isn't anyone like
you. You help the weak against the
strong. Lord our God, help us.
We trust in you."

2 Chronicles 14:11 NIRV

We can pray and trust God because He knows what is best for us. King Asa trusted in God because he knew that God would always help him.

When Asa became king, he saw that the people had not been worshipping God. They had disobeyed God's laws. King Asa knew that God was not pleased.

The king told the people they must worship God. He ordered them to obey God's laws. He told the people to trust God because God knew what was best for them.

Another king who lived in a nearby country did not want Asa's people to worship God. So King Asa knew he needed to gather an army of men. Some of the soldiers carried spears. Some carried bows and arrows. All of the men were very brave.

Finally the day came for the bad king and his soldiers to fight King Asa's army. King Asa knew he needed God's help to win the fight.

King Asa prayed, "Lord God, there is no one like You. We are weak but we know You can make us strong. So Lord God, help us. We trust in You. You are our God."

God heard King Asa's prayer. His soldiers won the fight.

Dear God, I'm so glad that You
always know what is best for
me. Help me to trust in You
when I feel very small and weak.
Amen.

The Battle Is the Lord's

"O our God, will you not judge them?
For we have no power to face this vast
army that is attacking us.
We do not know what to do, but our
eyes are upon you."

2 Chronicles 20:12

We can pray when we don't know what to do. Then we can do what Jehoshaphat did after he prayed—stand back and let God take care of things.

As soon as Jehoshaphat heard that the enemy army was coming, he was afraid. He knew he didn't have an army big enough to win the battle.

But Jehoshaphat had something bigger than an army. He had God, who could do anything. So he decided to ask God what he should do.

All the people came together to pray for God's help. They came from all the towns around. Jehoshaphat stood up among the people.

"Lord, You are the God of our

people," he prayed. "The enemy is coming, and we don't have the power to face this huge army. We do not know what to do, but we know You can help us."

One of the men standing nearby said, "King Jehoshaphat, listen! God has spoken to me. Do not be afraid. The battle is God's. He will take care of the great army."

The next day, Jehoshaphat and his men found that God had won the battle for them. Jehoshaphat and his men sang praises to God for answered prayers.

Dear God, sometimes I don't
know what to do.
Help me remember to pray and
then stand back and let
You take care of things.
Amen.

A Safe Trip

We [gave up eating] and prayed to our
God about our trip,
and he answered our prayers.

Ezra 8:23 NCV

We can pray for a safe trip whether we walk, ride our bikes, travel in a car, or fly in an airplane. Ezra and his people prayed for God to keep them safe on their trip.

A crowd of people stood by the river. They were packed and ready to go home. Ezra was the wise man who would show them the way.

"I could have asked the king for soldiers to guard us," Ezra told the people. "But I told the king that God would keep us safe. We will ask God to guard us. When we get home safely, it will show the king and the people that God takes care of those who love Him."

The next morning, before they left

for home, the people gathered together to pray. They prayed during the day as they walked. They prayed as they rested at night.

Day after day, they traveled. Sometimes they saw robbers hiding by the road, but God kept them safe. After many weeks, they finally reached their homes. God had answered their prayers. He kept them safe on their trip!

The next time your family goes on a trip, ask God to keep you all safe.

Dear God, I thank You
for loving me and taking care of
me. Thank You for keeping me
safe at all times—
no matter where I go.
Amen.

"Grant Me Favor"

"Give your servant success today
by granting him favor."
Nehemiah 1:11

We can pray when we are sad. Nehemiah prayed when he was sad, and God heard his prayer.

Nehemiah was a special helper to the king. He lived in a country far from his home and family. In those days, people would build strong walls around their towns. The walls kept out all kinds of dangers—fires, floods, wild animals, even big armies.

One day, Nehemiah's brother told him some sad news. "The walls of the city where we used to live are broken down. The city is not safe."

Nehemiah was sad. So Nehemiah prayed to God.

When the king saw Nehemiah, he

asked, "Why are you sad?"

"I am sad because the wall around the city where I used to live is broken down," Nehemiah answered. "I would like to go and help rebuild the wall around my town."

The king told Nehemiah, "You can go and help build the wall."

When Nehemiah came to the city, he met with the people. "We can work together to build the wall," he said. "We will make it strong again."

Bang, bang! Hammers and chisels cut the stone. *Zzzzz, zzzzz!* Saws cut the wood.

Soon the walls were fixed and the city was safe. God had heard Nehemiah's prayer.

Dear God, thank You for always
hearing my prayer.
Help me remember to pray
when I am sad. Help me to
remember that You can
make me happy again.
Amen.

"Why Is This Happening to Me?"

Job replied to the Lord,
"I know that you can do anything.
No one can keep you from doing what
you plan to do."
Job 42:1–2 NIRV

When we are having a bad day and everything seems to be going wrong, we can pray. Job had many bad days, but he kept on trusting God.

Did you have a bad day? Perhaps you fell and scraped your knee. Or you didn't get to go with your friends to the park. Maybe you didn't feel good. Some days are just like that!

Job obeyed God and God gave him many things—a big family, much land, many animals. God even kept Job from being sick. Job loved God and always did what was right.

One day, everything seemed to go wrong for Job. He lost his family and his animals. He got sick. Job didn't know why these things were happening.

"You must have done something wrong," said one of his friends.

"I have done nothing wrong," answered Job. "I love God and serve Him."

Then Job asked God, "Why is this happening to me?"

"Don't I know what is best for you?" answered God.

Then God did something that surprised Job and his friends. God made Job well. Then He gave him back everything he had lost—and much, much more.

Job trusted God even when things were going wrong!

Dear God, You know what is
best for me. Help me trust
in You when I'm having a bad
day and things go wrong.
I love You, God.
Amen.

"Hear Me When I Call"

The LORD will hear
when I call to him.
Psalm 4:3

God wants us to pray whenever we need His help. God chose David to be the new king—but even kings need help sometimes. He prayed that God would protect him and God answered his prayer.

Many people wanted to be king. Some people were jealous and angry when God chose David, especially old King Saul. He didn't want a young shepherd boy to take his place as king. He tried to kill David many times, but God kept David safe.

King Saul's men chased David, but God always showed David where to hide.

David hid from King Saul in the

desert. David hid in the hills. The old king and his men searched for him every day. But they could never find David.

One night, King Saul and his men were sleeping in a cave. They were tired. They had been chasing David all day long. David came quietly into the cave. He tiptoed over to where the king was sleeping. David could have killed Saul. But he knew God didn't want him to hurt the king.

Finally, King Saul died. David became king, just as God had planned.

What can you do when you are in trouble? You can pray to God and know that He will help you.

Dear God, thank You for helping
me when I'm in trouble.
Thank You for keeping me safe
just like You did for David.
Amen.

"Here Am I. Send Me!"

I heard the voice of the Lord saying, "Whom shall I send? And who will go for us?" And I said, "Here am I. Send me!"

Isaiah 6:8

God can talk to us when we pray. When God talks, He wants us to answer quickly. Isaiah was ready to answer when he heard God's voice.

Isaiah lived in a city where people were doing bad things. People had turned away from God. They were lying and stealing. They were saying things that were not pleasing to God. They did not worship God.

One day while Isaiah was worshipping in the temple, he heard God's voice say, "Whom shall I send to speak to these bad people?"

"Here am I. Send me!" said Isaiah.

God was pleased with Isaiah for answering Him quickly. God told Isaiah to go and tell the people to stop doing bad things. "Tell them to obey Me and do what is right," said God.

For many years, Isaiah asked the people to stop doing bad things and obey God. Isaiah warned the people what would happen if they kept disobeying. But only a few listened.

Isaiah was sad that the people did not want to obey and worship God.

But he was glad he had answered God's voice. He was doing what God had asked him to do.

Thank You, God, that I can
talk to You and hear what
You want to tell me. Help me
to always do what
You ask me to do.
Amen.

"I'm Only a Child"

"You are my Lord and King," [Jeremiah] said. "I don't know how to speak. I'm only a child."

Jeremiah 1:6 NIRV

Do you think you are too young to tell people about God? Then ask God to help you, just like Jeremiah did. He thought he was too young to speak to people about God, too.

The people God loved had forgotten Him. They no longer worshipped Him. God needed someone to take a message to His people.

One day, God spoke to young Jeremiah. "I want you to take My message to the people," said God. "Before you were born, I planned for you to speak for Me."

"But I'm so young," said Jeremiah. "I don't know how to speak to people."

"Don't worry about that," God said

to Jeremiah. "I'll tell you exactly what to say. There's no reason to be afraid."

Then God touched Jeremiah's mouth. God said, "Now you are ready. Just listen, and I will tell you just what to say."

Jeremiah got ready to tell the people God's message.

God spoke to Jeremiah again. "Do as I tell you. The people may not like what you tell them, but remember that I am with you. I will keep you safe."

Dear God, I know that
I am young, but I can tell
someone about You. Help me
to be brave and speak the
words You want me to say.
Amen.

One, Two, Three Times

Three times each day Daniel would
kneel down to pray and thank God,
just as he always had done.

Daniel 6:10 NCV

God hears us every time we pray. Daniel prayed—one, two, three times—every day, and God heard his prayer each time.

The king gave Daniel an important job. But some men did not like Daniel. They were jealous. They thought of a plan to get Daniel in trouble.

The men told the king, "Let's make a new rule. Everyone must pray to you." The king thought this rule was a good idea. He told the people they must pray only to him.

The next day, Daniel prayed to God—one, two, three times—just as he always did. The men, who were watching Daniel, ran to tell the king what they had seen.

The king was sad he had made the new rule. The men had tricked him. Now he had to throw Daniel into the lions' cage for disobeying the new rule.

The lions went r-r-roar! They were very hungry. R-r-roar!

But Daniel was not afraid. He knew God would take care of him.

The next morning the king came to the lions' cage. Daniel called out, "King, I am safe. God took care of me! He sent an angel to shut the lions' mouths."

The king made a new rule. Everyone should pray only to God.

Our heavenly Father, help me
to remember to pray when I'm
afraid. Keep me safe when I'm in
trouble. Thank You for hearing
my prayer every time I pray.
Amen.

Praying Anywhere

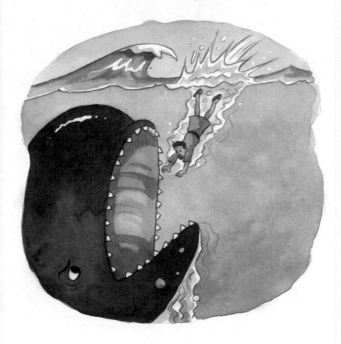

From inside the fish
Jonah prayed to the LORD his God.
Jonah 2:1

We can pray anywhere. Jonah prayed to God in many places—even from the inside of a fish!

One day God told Jonah, "Go to the town of Nineveh. Tell the people they have disobeyed Me."

Jonah had always obeyed God. But this time he disobeyed. Instead of going to Nineveh, he decided to get on a boat and go far away in the other direction.

Suddenly the sky turned black and strong winds blew. The waves crashed. The men on the boat were afraid. But Jonah knew God had sent the storm because he had disobeyed.

Jonah told the men, "Throw me into the sea and the storm will stop."

One, two, three! The men threw Jonah into the water. Sure enough, the waves stopped crashing. The boat was safe.

Then God sent a huge fish. The fish opened its mouth wide and *WHOOSH!* Jonah was in the belly of the big fish!

Jonah began to pray. "God, forgive me for disobeying."

When God brought the big fish close to land, it began to cough. *AACK!*—it coughed Jonah right onto the beach.

Then God talked to Jonah. "Now it's time to take My message to Nineveh!" And this time, Jonah obeyed!

Dear God, thank You for
hearing me when I pray at home,
at school, or at church.
I can pray anywhere,
and You will hear me.
Amen.

"Just Ask Believing"

"Just say the word, and my servant
will be healed."
Matthew 8:8

When we pray, we need to believe that God will answer our prayer. A soldier in the army believed that Jesus could answer a prayer. The soldier knew Jesus needed only to speak and his prayer would be answered.

Jesus was walking into the city of Capernaum. An important soldier ran to meet Him. "Jesus," the soldier said, "my helper is very sick. He cannot move and is in much pain." The soldier was worried because he was afraid his helper would die.

"I will come to your house and make your helper well," Jesus said.

"No, Jesus. I can see how busy You are," the soldier said. "You do not need to come all the way to my house. If You will just say that my helper is well, I know that he will be healed."

Jesus was surprised. He turned to the people who were with Him. "This man believes in Me more than anyone," He said.

Then Jesus turned to the soldier. "Go home," He said. "Because you believe in Me, your helper is already over his sickness."

When the soldier returned home, he found his helper completely well. The soldier had believed that Jesus could answer his prayer.

Dear Jesus, help me believe that
You can answer my prayers—
even when I cannot see You
answering them. Thank You for
caring for me and loving me.
Amen.

"Lord, Save Us!"

The disciples went and woke him,
saying, "Lord, save us!
We're going to drown!"
Matthew 8:25

When we are afraid, we can pray. One time, Jesus' disciples prayed when they were caught in a bad storm.

Jesus had been teaching people about God. He was very tired from His busy day.

He and His disciples climbed into a small fishing boat and sailed onto the lake. Jesus was so tired that He went to the back of the boat and laid down for a nap.

Suddenly, a storm came up. The wind began to blow. The waves rocked the boat. The wind and the waves made it hard for the disciples to stand up. The boat was beginning to fill with water.

Even though some of the disciples

were big, strong fishermen, they were afraid. They woke Jesus and said, "Lord, save us! We are going to drown!"

"Why are you afraid?" Jesus asked. "Don't you know I will always take care of you—no matter how bad the storm gets?"

Jesus stood up and stretched out His arms. He told the wind to stop blowing. He told the waves to be still and stop rocking the boat. Suddenly, everything was quiet.

The disciples were surprised that Jesus could make the storm obey Him. They were no longer afraid.

Dear God, Thank You for always being nearby, watching over me. When I'm afraid, help me to remember that You are taking care of me. Amen.

"Have Mercy on Us"

As Jesus went on from there,
two blind men followed him, calling
out, "Have mercy on us, Son of David!"
Matthew 9:27

Jesus wants us to pray about everything—big things and small things. Two blind men believed that Jesus could make them see again, and Jesus heard their prayer.

Everywhere in the town, people were talking about Jesus and His miracles. Crowds of people started following Him around, trying to hear what He had to say.

At the end of the day, Jesus was tired and wanted to rest. Step, step, step went Jesus' sandals as He walked toward the house where He would spend the night.

Swish, swish, swish! Two blind men slowly moved along behind Him. They called out to Jesus, "Have mercy on us, Son of David!"

Jesus went into the house and the two blind men followed. When Jesus turned around, He saw the blind men. "Do you believe that I can do this?" He asked them.

"Yes, Lord, we believe," they said.

Jesus touched their eyes and said, "If you believe, it will happen to you."

Suddenly, the blind men could see. Jesus had heard their prayer. Jesus told them not to tell anyone what happened. But they were too happy for that. They told everyone they met that Jesus had touched their eyes—and now they could see.

Jesus, I believe in You! I know
that You can do anything—
big things and small things.
Help me remember to pray
when I need Your help.
Amen.

Loaves and Fish

[Jesus] took the five loaves and the two fish and, looking to heaven, he thanked God for the food.

Matthew 14:19 NCV

God wants us to thank Him for the food we eat—just like Jesus did.

Jesus and His disciples sat down to rest on a hillside one day. Before they knew it, a lot of people had gathered around. They wanted Jesus to tell them about God.

Jesus started to teach them. Soon, many people were sitting on the grassy hill, listening to Him. They listened until suppertime. They didn't even notice they were hungry until Jesus stopped talking.

"We should send these people home so they can eat supper," Jesus' disciples said to Him.

But Jesus said to His disciples,

"They are too far from home. We must give them something to eat."

"What?" the disciples said. "We don't have any food!"

Just then Andrew said, "This little boy says he wants to share his supper. But it is only five little loaves of bread and two fish. It is enough to feed only a few."

Jesus took the little boy's supper and thanked God for the food. Then He began to break the bread and fish into pieces. Soon there were hundreds and hundreds of pieces of bread and fish— enough to feed all the hungry people.

Heavenly Father, thank You
for giving me food to eat.
Help me to share my food
with those who are hungry.
Amen.

"Lord, Save Me!"

When [Peter] saw the wind,
he was afraid and, beginning to sink,
cried out, "Lord, save me!"
Matthew 14:30

Prayers don't have to be long. One time, Peter, one of Jesus' helpers, prayed a prayer that only had three words. And God answered that prayer!

Peter and eleven other men—Jesus' helpers—were in a boat. They were tired because they had just helped Jesus feed thousands of people. They were still talking about the miracle Jesus had done when He fed all those people with only five loaves of bread and two little fish.

The wind started to blow. *Whish!* The waves got bigger! Jesus' helpers were working hard to keep the water out of the boat, when someone yelled.

"It's a ghost!" they shouted. They were all afraid. Who was that walking toward them on the water?

"It's Me," said Jesus. "Don't be afraid."

Brave Peter said, "Lord, if it's You, tell me to come to You."

"Come," said Jesus.

Peter did something surprising! He stepped over the side of the boat and walked on the water!

Then Peter saw how big the waves were and how hard the wind was blowing. He looked away from Jesus and began to sink. "Lord, save me!" he prayed.

Jesus caught Peter's hand and helped him into the boat. Peter was glad his three-word prayer was answered.

Dear Jesus, help me not to be
afraid when storms come,
but to believe that You will
take care of me. Thank You for
hearing all my prayers.
Amen.

"Hosanna in the Highest!"

"Hosanna to the Son of David!"
"Blessed is he who comes in the name
of the Lord!" "Hosanna in the highest!"
Matthew 21:9

Praising God is part of praying. The people sang praises to Jesus as He came into the city of Jerusalem.

Step, step, step! Jesus and His special helpers were going to the temple. On the way, Jesus stopped and said, "There is a little donkey in the city. Untie it and bring it to Me."

Jesus' helpers did just as He asked them. They found the donkey and brought it back to Jesus. Jesus climbed on the donkey's back and rode it into the city.

Clippety-clop, clippety-clop went the donkey's feet. Jesus' helpers walked along the road beside Him.

Many other people were walking

along the road. They were happy to see Jesus!

Some people spread their coats on the road. Other people cut branches from palm trees and laid them on the road. This showed that they believed that Jesus was a real, true king.

Some other people ran ahead to the city. "Jesus is coming! Jesus is coming!" they shouted. When they heard the shouts, still more people came to see Jesus. They sang praises to Him, "Hosanna! Hosanna in the highest!"

What a happy day it was! Everyone who loved Jesus praised Him by singing happy songs.

Thank You, God, for sending
Your Son, Jesus. Help me to be
happy and show my love to Jesus
by singing praises. Help me tell
others about Jesus' love.
Amen.

"She Is Only Sleeping"

Get up.

[Jairus] begged Jesus, "Please come.
My little daughter is dying.
Place your hands on her to heal her.
Then she will live."

Mark 5:23 NIRV

Jesus wants us to pray and tell Him about our sick friends and family. Jesus listened to Jairus and made his daughter well—even when people didn't think He could.

Splish, splash went the water as Jesus stepped off the boat and onto the shore. When Jairus saw Jesus, he came running to Him and bowed down.

"My little daughter is very sick," Jairus told Jesus. "Please come and put Your hands on her. Then she will be made well."

On the way to Jairus's house, a man came running toward them. "Don't bother Jesus," he said to Jairus. "Your little girl died."

Jesus kept walking. "Don't be afraid," he told Jairus. "Trust Me. She is only sleeping."

When Jesus reached Jairus's house, He saw the little girl lying on the bed. Her eyes were closed. She was very still.

Jesus took her by the hand and said, "Little girl, listen to Me. Get up!"

All of a sudden, the little girl's eyes opened. She stood up and walked around.

Jesus turned to the girl's mother and said, "I think she's hungry. Give her something to eat."

Jesus knew He could make Jairus's daughter well—and He did!

Thank You, Jesus, for keeping me well. When my friends or family members are sick, help me remember to tell You about them. You can make them well. Amen.

A Silent Prayer

She thought, "I just need to touch his clothes. Then I will be healed."

Mark 5:28 NIRV

Sometimes we pray aloud and sometimes we think a prayer. Jesus hears every prayer—the ones we think and the ones we say out loud. Jesus heard a prayer from a woman that no one else heard.

Everywhere Jesus went, a crowd of people followed Him. Some wanted Jesus to make them well, and some wanted Jesus to tell them more about God.

In the crowd one day was a woman who had been sick for twelve years. She had been to many doctors, but they could not make her well. She was not getting better. She heard about Jesus and wanted to see if He could help her.

"I just need to touch His clothes,"

she thought. "Then I will be healed."

Suddenly, the woman reached out and touched Jesus' clothes. Something wonderful happened! The sickness left her.

No one had heard her prayer. No one—but Jesus! He turned and looked into the crowd. "Who touched Me?" He asked.

Then the woman came and fell at His feet. She was shaking with fear, but she told Jesus what she had done.

Jesus said to her, "Dear woman, you believed in Me and you are made well."

Dear Jesus, thank You for
hearing my prayers—
whether I think them or
say them out loud.
Help me remember that You
can do all things.
Amen.

"I Do Believe!"

Immediately the father cried out, "I do believe! Help me to believe more!"

Mark 9:24 NCV

God wants us to believe with all our hearts that He will answer our prayers. He waited for one worried dad to say the words before He healed his son.

There was a big crowd of people around Jesus. They wanted to hear what He had to say. In the crowd was a man with a sick boy, who wanted to talk to Jesus.

"I brought my son to You," he said to Jesus. "He cannot hear or speak. I asked Your special helpers to make him well, but they could not."

"How long has your boy had this sickness?" asked Jesus.

"Since he was a young child," answered the father. "I love him so much. If You can do anything, show us kindness. Please help us."

"Do you believe that I can make your boy well?" Jesus asked. "Anything is possible if you believe."

Tears came to the father's eyes. Right away he said, "I do believe! Help me to believe more!"

Then Jesus looked at the boy. "Sickness, come out and never go back in again!" He commanded.

The boy was completely healed when his dad said the words "I believe!"

Thank You, Jesus, for answering
my prayers. Help me believe in
You with all my heart.
Amen.

"Have Mercy on Me!"

[Bartimaeus] began to shout, "Jesus, Son of David, have mercy on me!"
Mark 10:47

Sometimes we pray for a big miracle. Sometimes we pray for a small miracle. Bartimaeus received a big miracle from Jesus.

Bartimaeus sat by the roadside. He felt the soft grass, but he could not see it. He heard the birds singing, but he could not see them.

One day, Bartimaeus heard people shouting, "Jesus is coming!" He heard the *swish*, *swish* of Jesus' sandals, but he could not see Him. Bartimaeus was blind.

He began to shout, "Jesus, Jesus!"

The people standing nearby said, "Be quiet."

But Bartimaeus shouted louder,

"Jesus, have mercy on me!"

Jesus stopped. He told the people to bring the blind man to Him. The people called to Bartimaeus, "Get up! Jesus is calling you."

Bartimaeus threw off his coat and jumped to his feet. He moved toward Jesus.

Jesus looked at the blind man and asked, "What do you want Me to do?"

"Please help me see," answered Bartimaeus.

Jesus said to him, "Go. You are able to see now."

Bartimaeus's eyes were opened. He saw the blue sky above and the birds sitting in the branches of the trees. He saw the people. "I can see! I can see!" he shouted as he followed Jesus down the road.

Dear God, thank You for giving me eyes to see the beautiful world You have made. Help me to be thankful for miracles—big ones and small ones. Amen.

Thank You for Sending Jesus

[Anna] gave thanks to God
and spoke about the child to all.
Luke 2:38

When we pray, we can thank God for sending His Son, Jesus. Anna thanked God when she saw the baby Jesus.

Step, step, step. Mary held the baby Jesus close as she walked up the big steps to the temple. Step, step, step. Joseph walked beside Mary. They were taking baby Jesus to the temple for the very first time. Mary held Jesus gently in her arms as they gave their offerings and prayed.

There was a woman named Anna in the temple. She was very old. She had lived in the temple most of her life. Every day, she prayed and served God.

When Anna saw the baby Jesus, she knew that He was God's Son.

"Look! Look everybody!" she said, pointing to the baby. "This baby is Jesus, God's Son!"

Anna moved closer to Mary and Joseph. She looked at Jesus and prayed. "Thank You, God, for sending Jesus, Your Son. Thank You for letting me see baby Jesus!"

Anna was so happy that she had seen the baby Jesus. She told others about seeing God's Son.

When she gave thanks to God, her words became a prayer of praise to Him.

Dear God, thank You for
sending Your Son, Jesus.
Thank you for the people who
tell me about Him. Help me
to tell others about
Your Son, Jesus.
Amen.

Mary's Song

Mary said, "My soul praises the Lord."
Luke 1:46 NCV

Praising God is an important part of prayer. Mary praised God when she learned she was going to be the mother of God's Son.

After the angel Gabriel left Mary, she thought about the good news he had told her: "God has chosen you from all the women in the world," the angel had said. "You will have a baby boy. He will be the Son of God. You will call His name Jesus. He will be great."

Mary was happy. She wanted to share her good news with her cousin, Elizabeth. Mary hurried to Elizabeth's house. How glad the women were to see each other. They shared the good news.

"I'm glad you have come to visit

me," Elizabeth told Mary. "I am happy that the mother of God's Son has come to my house."

Mary was happy, too. She was so happy that she praised God with a beautiful song. "My heart is full of praise for God," Mary sang. "He has made me happy. God has remembered me, even though I'm not very important. From now until the end of time, all people will call me blessed because God has done wonderful things for me. God is good. He loves us all!"

Dear God, I'm so happy
You love me. Thank You for
all the wonderful things You
have given me, but most of all,
thank You for sending
Your Son, Jesus.
Amen.

Ask Jesus to Help

[Peter's] mother-in-law was suffering
from a high fever,
and they asked Jesus to help her.
Luke 4:38

When we pray for the sick, Jesus will help them. Simon Peter asked for help when his wife's mother got sick with a fever.

Jesus had been teaching the people about God, His Father, all day long. When He finished, He looked around. "Where is Simon Peter?" Jesus asked the other disciples.

Swish, swish went Jesus' sandals as He walked to Peter's house. When He got there, He found Peter waiting.

"Please, Jesus, pray for my wife's mother. She is so sick. Can You make her well again?" Simon asked.

Jesus stood by the woman's bed. He looked down at her and prayed for her.

Suddenly, her fever went away. She got out of bed and said she had work to do in the kitchen. Everyone was surprised.

When the neighbors heard what Jesus had done, they brought all the sick people in their families to Jesus. He gently touched each one. Just like that, they were well again.

Finally, Jesus went away to rest. He was very tired. But other people came with their sick loved ones. They searched for Jesus until they found Him.

Dear Jesus, help me remember
to pray for people who are sick.
I know You can make them well
again. Thank You for making me
well when I am sick.
Amen.

"I Need Some Men to Help Me"

One of those days Jesus went out
to a mountainside to pray,
and spent the night praying to God.
Luke 6:12

God wants us to pray whenever we need something. Jesus did that when He asked God to send Him some helpers.

Jesus was tired. He walked up the mountain and found a cool place to sit down and rest. All day, Jesus had been busy helping sick people. He had told many moms and dads about God's love. But still many, many people were sick. More moms and dads needed to know about God's love. Jesus wanted to help every person.

Jesus prayed all night. He asked God to help Him choose twelve special helpers.

The next morning as the bright sun began to warm the earth, Jesus knew what God wanted Him to do. He called all His friends together.

"I need some men to help Me," Jesus told the friends. "I'm going to choose some special helpers." He chose a man named Peter and his brother, Andrew. He chose two more men who were brothers, James and John. Jesus asked other men to be His special helpers, too—until there were twelve.

After that, Jesus always took His special helpers with Him to help Him pray for all the people who needed help.

Jesus was glad that He had talked with God about the men He chose to help Him.

Thank You, Jesus, for always
helping me when I have
to choose. I don't know how
to pick but You do.
Amen.

"Tell My Sister to Help Me!"

[Martha] came to him and asked,
"Lord, don't you care that my sister has
left me to do the work by myself?
Tell her to help me!"
Luke 10:40

Jesus wants us to stop our work and play, and spend time in prayer with Him. Martha complained about all the work she had to do. But Jesus told her what was more important.

Jesus had three special friends who lived in the town of Bethany. Whenever Jesus was in that town, He would stop at the house of His friends, Mary, Martha, and Lazarus.

One day Jesus stopped in the town, and Martha saw Him. "Come, stay at our house," she told Jesus.

Jesus came to Martha's house. Martha's sister, Mary, was pleased to see Jesus. She sat on the floor by His feet and listened to every word He said.

While Mary sat and listened to Jesus, Martha was working. She was planning a special meal. She wanted Jesus to enjoy His time with them.

Martha was upset because Mary was not helping her. Martha spoke to Jesus, "My sister is letting me do all the work. Tell Mary to help me!"

Jesus looked at Martha and said, "Martha, you are too worried about little things.

Mary has chosen to do the most important thing. She has chosen to listen to Me."

Dear Jesus, thank You for being my friend. Help me to remember the most important thing— and that is to spend time talking and listening to You.

Amen.

"Lord, Teach Us to Pray"

One day Jesus was praying in a certain place. When he finished, one of his disciples said to him, "Lord, teach us to pray."

Luke 11:1

Praying is talking to God, just like you would talk to anyone else. God wants to know the things you need. But He also wants to know the fun things you do. Jesus' disciples wanted to know how to pray, and Jesus taught them.

Jesus spent much time praying to God. Sometimes He would stay awake all night to pray. Sometimes Jesus would find a quiet spot where He could talk to God.

Jesus' special helpers, the disciples, saw Jesus pray many times. One day when Jesus had finished praying, one of the disciples came to Him. The disciple said, "Jesus, teach us how to pray."

Jesus told His helpers that they

could talk to God the same way they talked to their fathers here on earth.

Jesus said, "When you pray, call God, 'Father.' Tell Him you love Him. Ask Him for the food you need each day. Ask Him to forgive the wrong things you do. Tell Him that you will forgive people who have done bad things to you. Ask Him to help you do what is right."

Jesus was happy because His disciples wanted to know how to talk to God. He is happy when you talk to God, too!

Heavenly Father, thank You for
listening to me when I pray.
I'm glad I can tell You what
I need, but I'm also happy
I can tell You about the
fun things, too.
Amen.

She Praised Him

[Jesus] put his hands on her,
and immediately she straightened
up and praised God.

Luke 13:13

Praising God means that we are thanking God for the things He gives us and the things He does for us. A woman with a crooked back praised God for making her back straight again.

Tap, tap, tap went the cane as the woman walked along the street toward the temple. Step, step, step went the other people hurrying past her.

For many years, the woman had not been able to stand straight and tall. She walked slowly and used a walking cane to help her.

Tap, tap, tap. The woman climbed the steps of the temple with her cane.

She was happy to be at church because she wanted to hear Jesus read from the Bible. She listened to Jesus teach.

As Jesus looked at the crowd of people in the temple, He saw the woman with a crooked back. Jesus asked the woman to come to Him. Gently, He touched her back. "Now, your back is well. Strong and straight," said Jesus.

The woman looked very surprised. She stood up straight. She let her cane drop to the floor and raised her arms high above her head.

The woman's face was lit up with a smile as she thanked God for making her well.

Dear God, the woman said thank You. I can say thank You, too, for all the things You do for me. You are a great God and I love You. Amen.

Saying Thank You

[One of the men] bowed down at Jesus'
feet and thanked him.

Luke 17:16 NCV

Do you remember to thank God for making you well after you have been sick? A sick man, who was made well, almost forgot to thank Jesus.

There was a man who had sores all over his body. He was sad because he had to leave his family and go to a place where nine other sick men lived.

One day, Jesus came down the road. "Please make us well!" the sick men called out to Jesus.

Jesus saw the sores on the men's hands and feet. "Go and show yourselves to the helpers at the temple," He said.

The ten men were happy! They ran down the road toward town. Suddenly, they looked at their hands and feet. The sores were gone! Jesus had made them well.

The men ran faster toward the temple—all but one man. He stopped and ran back to Jesus. The man got down on his knees in front of Jesus. He said, "Thank You for making me well!"

Jesus looked at the man and said, "I'm glad you came back to thank Me. Go home to your family. You knew I could make you well and I did."

Dear heavenly Father,
whenever I am sick, help me to
remember to thank You for
making me well again.
Amen.

"Father, Forgive Them"

Jesus said, "Father, forgive them, for
they do not know what they are doing."
Luke 23:34

We can pray and ask Jesus to forgive us when we do wrong things. Jesus even forgave the men who did bad things to Him.

When Jesus came down to earth from heaven, some people didn't like Him. They treated Him very badly. But Jesus didn't get mad. He prayed, "Father, forgive them, for they don't know what they are doing. They don't know that I'm Your Son."

Other people knew right away that Jesus was God's Son. They loved Him and followed Him. They listened to Him as He taught them about the heavenly Father.

Jesus told them that His heavenly

Father was their Father, too. He assured them that He was kind and gentle and forgiving.

Has anyone ever treated you un-kindly? Did they hurt you with their words or the things they did? Ask God to forgive them, just like Jesus did.

And when you do wrong things, you can go to Jesus, too. He won't be angry. He'll say, "Come on in, My little child. I'm glad you are sorry for what you've done wrong. I forgive you because I love you so much."

Dear Jesus, You forgave people
even when they were hurting
You. Help me remember that
when I do wrong, I hurt You,
too. Forgive me when I sin.
Amen.

Begging for Help

When this man heard that Jesus had
arrived in Galilee from Judea,
he went to him and begged him to
come and heal his son,
who was close to death.

John 4:47

When we pray, we can believe that Jesus will answer our prayer. It took a miracle for one of the king's soldiers to believe in Jesus and know his prayers would be answered.

Jesus was in a town called Cana— where He did his first miracle. When the king's soldier learned that Jesus was in his city, he hurried to Him. "Please heal my son," begged the soldier. "He is very sick."

Jesus said to the soldier, "Unless I give you a miracle, you will never believe in Me."

"Sir, come before my son dies," begged the soldier again.

Jesus looked at the man and

answered him. "Go on home. Your son is already well."

The soldier believed what Jesus told him and started home. A man from home met him on the way and said, "I came to tell you your son is fine. It's a miracle!"

"What time did he get well?" the soldier asked.

"He had a bad fever. Then at one o'clock the fever was gone," the man answered.

The soldier knew that one o'clock was the exact time that Jesus told him his son was better. So the soldier and his family believed in Jesus.

Thank You, Jesus, for always
answering my prayers.
Help me to remember that
I can pray when people in my
family are sick, and
believe that You will make
them better
Amen.

"I Have No One to Help Me"

The sick man answered, "Sir, there is no
one to help me get into the pool."
John 5:7 NCV

Sometimes when we pray, God sends someone to help answer our prayer. The man who could not walk needed help, and Jesus came to help him.

Swish, swish went the water in the pool. When the water started moving, a sick person could get into the pool and, just like magic, that person would be well. But the magic would only work one time! So many people were waiting. Some were blind and some were crippled or sick. They all sat by the side of the pool, watching. They all wanted to be the first person to jump in when the water began to swish.

One day Jesus walked by. He saw a

man who had been lying near the pool for many, many years. "Do you want to be well?" Jesus asked the man.

"Oh, yes," the sick man answered. "But I'm too slow, and I have no one to help me. Someone else always gets into the swishing water before me."

Then Jesus said, "Stand up. Pick up your mat and walk."

Suddenly, the man was well. He picked up his mat and began to walk. The man was happy that Jesus made him well.

Thank You, Jesus, for helping me
get well when I am sick.
Thank You for my family, who
helps me when I am sick.
Thank You for doctors, too.
Amen.

Praying for Self, Family, and Others

After Jesus said this,
he looked toward heaven and prayed.
John 17:1

God wants us to pray for ourselves, our families, and others. Jesus gave us an example. He prayed for Himself, His disciples, and then for all those who believed in Him.

Jesus was talking to His disciples. He wanted to help them understand that soon He would go to heaven. He reminded His followers that God had sent Him to earth to tell them about God's great love for them.

After Jesus had talked to His disciples, He began to pray. First of all, He prayed for Himself. He told God that He had finished the work that He had been sent to do on earth. He said He was ready to go to heaven.

Then Jesus prayed for His followers. "Dear Father," He prayed. "When I am gone, please help My followers. I have told them all about You. They will tell others. Keep them safe."

Then Jesus continued praying. "God, please help all people who believe in Me. Keep all these people close to You. Help them to love and help each other."

Jesus finished His prayer. He prayed for Himself and His disciples. He prayed for all believers—even those who had not yet been born.

God, thank You for showing me how to pray. Help me to pray— not just for myself and the things I need but also for my family and others.
Amen.

"Hear Our Prayer, O Lord"

They all came together regularly to pray.

Acts 1:14 NIRV

We can pray with our family every day, and we can pray with others at church each week. After Jesus went to heaven, His special helpers found out how important it was to pray together.

Jesus' special helpers didn't know what to do without Jesus. It seemed like they were all alone. They felt lonely and afraid.

One day, the helpers went upstairs to the room where they were staying. They remembered that Jesus had told them how important it was to pray and talk to God. So the helpers decided that every day, they would pray right there in that room, for themselves and for others.

Soon some women came to pray with them. Jesus' mother, Mary, and His brothers came, too. Other people who believed in Jesus heard and came to the upstairs room to pray.

The people prayed for the sick and those who needed help. They prayed for God to keep them safe. They prayed for those who wanted to hurt them. By praying, they learned what God wanted them to do and how they could tell others about Jesus.

Every day more people came to pray. They learned that when they prayed together they no longer felt lonely or afraid.

Dear God, thank You that I can
pray with my family every day.
Thank You for my church where
I can go and pray with
my friends.
Amen.

Special Helpers

They presented these men to the
apostles, who prayed and laid their
hands on them.

Acts 6:6

We should remember to pray for the special helpers at church.

Every day, Jesus' friends told more and more people that Jesus loved them. More and more people learned to love Jesus. Every day, these people shared their food and clothing with those who didn't have any.

But one day, some women whose husbands had died said to the others, "No one is sharing food with us. We are not getting enough to eat! Please help us with this problem."

When Jesus' friends heard about this, they were sad. They wanted everyone to have enough food to eat. But they were too busy telling people about

Jesus to cook the dinners themselves. They bowed their heads and asked God what to do.

Jesus' friends gathered everyone.

"We know it isn't fair that some people don't get enough food to eat," Jesus' friends said. "This is what we will do. Choose seven special helpers. These special helpers will make sure everyone gets enough food."

So the people chose one, two, three, four, five, six, seven men to be special helpers. Then Jesus' friends prayed and asked God to help the seven men to take care of all the people.

Dear God, thank You for the
special helpers in my church.
Help me to remember to pray
for them. Help me to share
with others, too.
Amen.

"Who Are You, Lord?"

Who are you, Lord?

"Who are you, Lord?" Saul asked.
Acts 9:5

There was an important man in town named Saul. He said that he loved and respected God. But he did not think that Jesus was God's Son. Saul was angry that so many people were following Jesus! He did his best to keep them from telling others about Jesus.

"I will go to other cities and stop people from talking about Jesus," Saul said. "I will put them in jail if I have to!" Saul and his friends got on their horses and headed for a city called Damascus.

On the road, Saul and his friends saw a very bright light. Saul was shocked and surprised! He fell to the ground. The light was so bright that Saul could not see anything!

Then Saul heard a voice, "Saul, why are you hurting Me?"

"Who are You?" asked Saul.

The voice said, "I am Jesus, the one you are hurting."

Then Saul's friends took him to the house of a man who loved Jesus. For three days, Saul stayed there and prayed.

God sent a man to find Saul and pray for him. Suddenly, Saul could see again! He was so sorry that he had hurt those who loved Jesus. He began telling people that Jesus was God's Son.

Dear Jesus, I love You.
Thank You for loving me. Help
me to obey You and to tell other
people that You love them, too.
Amen.

"Dorcas, Get Up!"

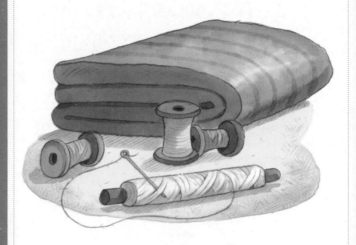

Peter sent them all out of the room;
then he got down on his knees
and prayed.

Acts 9:40

Sometimes people who do nice things get sick. We can pray for them just as Peter did for Dorcas.

Dorcas was a kind woman who loved Jesus. She wanted to help people. One way she helped was by sewing clothes for people who needed them. The people loved Dorcas very much.

One day, Dorcas became very sick. Her friends were sad. They didn't know what to do.

"Peter could help us," said one of Dorcas's friends. "Let's go ask him to pray for her."

Two men hurried to find Peter. "Come quickly!" they said when they found him.

When Peter arrived at Dorcas's house, he went upstairs to the room where she was in bed. Dorcas's friends were in the room, crying. They showed Peter the clothes she had made for them. Peter saw how much the women loved Dorcas.

Peter said, "Please leave the room for a moment."

Then Peter knelt beside Dorcas and prayed. He talked to God about Dorcas and her friends. After Peter prayed for God's help, he called out, "Dorcas, get up!"

Just like that, Dorcas opened her eyes and got up! Peter called to her friends, and they came and saw Dorcas. She was standing and smiling at them! God had answered Peter's prayer.

Dear God, thank You for giving
me special people who do nice
things for me. Help me remember
to pray for them when they
are sick or need help.
Amen.

"What Is It, Lord?"

Cornelius and all his family were
faithful and worshiped God.
He gave freely to people who were in
need. He prayed to God regularly.
Acts 10:2 NIRV

We can pray for people who go to faraway places and tell people about Jesus. Even though Cornelius prayed and gave offerings to God, he did not know about Jesus until God sent someone to tell him.

One day, God sent an angel to Cornelius. When he saw the angel, Cornelius was afraid. "What is it, Lord?" he asked.

The angel answered, "God has heard your prayers and knows you give money to help others. God wants you to bring Peter to your house. He has something important to tell you." Cornelius sent messengers to find Peter right away.

Even before the messengers came,

God had spoken to Peter about going to faraway places and telling people about Jesus.

"Cornelius sent us to get you," the messengers told Peter. "An angel told Cornelius to invite you to his house. He wants to hear what you have to say."

Peter knew that God wanted him to go to Cornelius's house. It was a long trip but he didn't mind.

When Peter arrived at the house, he found Cornelius and his family waiting. Peter told them about Jesus. Cornelius and his family heard about Jesus for the first time.

Thank You, God, for the people
who tell me about Jesus.
Help the people You send to
faraway places to tell boys
and girls about You.
Amen.

The Church Prayed

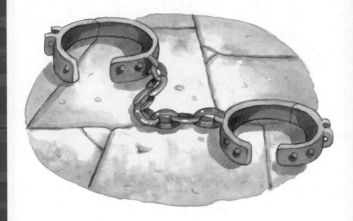

Peter was kept in prison.
But the church prayed hard
to God for him.

Acts 12:5 NIRV

God wants us to pray for those who are in trouble.

Peter was telling people—anyone who would listen—about Jesus. Soon soldiers came along and put him in prison. They said it was against the law to talk about Jesus.

All Peter's church friends got together to pray for him. They prayed a long time. They asked God to help Peter.

In the middle of the night, while Peter was sleeping, God sent an angel.

"Quick, get up!" the angel said.

Swish, swish! Peter followed the angel past the sleeping guards. *Clink, clink!* The gate opened. *Clack, clack!*

Peter and the angel walked outside into the street.

Suddenly, the angel was gone. Peter knew that God had freed him. He walked to the house where his church friends were praying.

Knock, knock! Peter rapped on the door. A girl named Rhoda came to the door and asked, "Who is it?"

"It's me," said Peter.

Rhoda knew his voice. She knew it was Peter. She was so excited she forgot to open the door. She ran back to the people who were praying. "Peter is here!" she shouted. Everyone stopped praying and ran to the door. God had answered their prayers!

Dear God in heaven, remind me
to pray for others when
they are in trouble and need
Your help. Thank You for
always answering my prayers.
Amen.

Thank You for My Church

On the Sabbath we went outside the
city gate to the river, where we expected
to find a place of prayer.

Acts 16:13

We can thank God for our church where we can pray and sing praises to God. Paul and his friends were happy to find a place to worship—even though it was on the riverbank.

Clack, clack, clack went the sandals as Paul and his friends walked into town. They saw many buildings but they could not find a church building where people could worship God.

Paul heard about a group of people who gathered beside the river to sing songs and pray. So when it was time for church, Paul and his friends looked for the group beside the river.

Clack, clack, clack. Out of town and down the road went Paul and his friends. Before long, they saw the river. And there, under the big shade tree was a group of women. They were praying, and singing praise songs. Paul and his friends spoke to the women.

One of the women was named Lydia. She loved God, but she had never heard about Jesus. As Paul talked, Lydia listened closely. She knew what Paul was telling her was very important. Lydia was happy that Paul had found the river church and told her about Jesus.

Dear God, thank You for my church where I can sing songs and hear stories from the Bible. Thank You for people who love me and take me to church.

Amen.

Praying and Singing

About midnight Paul and Silas were
praying and singing hymns to God.
Acts 16:25

God hears our prayers, no matter where we are or what time it is. Paul and Silas knew God heard their prayers—even in jail in the middle of the night.

One day, Paul and Silas were telling people about Jesus. Some people were glad to hear about Jesus, but others became angry. They shouted, "Put Paul and Silas in jail! Do not let them out!"

The jailer put Paul and Silas in the back of the jail. He put chains around their hands and feet. They could hardly move. It was very dark and quiet.

In the middle of the night, Paul and Silas prayed. They began to sing praises to God. The prayers made Paul and Silas happy. The songs made them happy, too.

Suddenly, there were loud noises! *Bang! Crash!* Everything began to shake. It was an earthquake! The earthquake popped open the jail doors. It shook loose the chains around Paul and Silas.

The jailer was afraid. "Paul and Silas have escaped!" he yelled.

But Paul said, "We're still here." Then Paul and Silas told the jailer about Jesus. Paul and Silas were happy because God had heard their prayers and their singing—even in jail in the middle of the night!

Dear Jesus, thank You for being near me at all times. Help me remember to pray and sing praises to You wherever I am and at anytime—day or night. Amen.

"Don't Be Afraid, Pray"

"Keep up your courage, men,
for I [Paul] have faith in God
that it will happen just as he told me."

Acts 27:25

God wants us to pray when we are afraid. Paul prayed when he was on a ship during a strong storm. But he knew God would keep him and all the other passengers safe.

Paul saw the sky grow dark and cloudy. He felt the wind blow harder and harder. Soon the ship was in terrible trouble. The howling wind blew the ship farther out to sea. It tossed up and down on huge waves.

Paul and the others were afraid the ship would sink. Waves crashed over the deck. Salty water splashed in their faces.

Paul prayed and prayed and prayed.

The storm lasted for many days.

The men were getting hungry. They were very scared. Everyone thought they would drown—everyone except Paul.

Paul knew God wanted him to tell many more people about Jesus. Paul told the frightened men, "Do not be afraid. God says He will take care of us. Everyone will be safe."

Suddenly the ship hit rocks and broke into pieces. Some of the men swam to the beach. Others floated to the beach on pieces of wood. But everyone got there safely.

Thank You, God, for being near me and keeping me safe at all times. When I am afraid, help me remember that You are always taking care of me. Amen.

Jane Landreth enjoys touching young lives with God's love. She taught school until the birth of her son, then officially launched her writing career using her son's adventures for story ideas. Jane and her husband, Jack, reside in the Ozarks, where she writes for children and teaches writing for a distance-learning school.

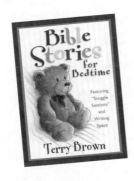